Ferrying the Stars

Half Inch Press

ISBN 978-1-969849-08-4

Ferrying the Stars

Justin Hollis

Acknowledgements

Many of these poems have appeared in the following magazines: *Action Spectacle, Chiron Review, Cholla Needles, Corpus Callosum, Eunoia Review, GAS: Poetry, Art, and Music, Home Planet News, Main Street Rag, Querencia Press Quarterly Anthology,* and *Superpresent.*

*

The cover is an altered image of *Main Street of the Yoshiwara on a Starlight Night* (1852-64) by Utagawa Kunisada II.

Contents

61 / The movie hadn't started
62 / The TV weatherman
63 / It is time to cut the cake
64 / In my childhood bedroom
65 / I'm asked to check my squirt pistol
66 / More and more now
67 / All the men in the photo
68 / My son is telling me
69 / I'm out for a walk
70 / It is so pleasant
71 / It was a sultry
72 / We were square dancing
73 / He turns the crank
74 / We are about to pull the plug
75 / I am exploring Mars

1

A snail shell with monster truck tires. Tank treads on a lion seal. They rev their engines at the finish line, race backwards to the beginning, where the clubfooted mayor in a two-piece bikini waits to present the trophy cup to the victor. I watch the action through the living room window, grandmother bouncing on my knee. For every blind turn the competitors navigate without crashing she grows a little younger, until she is nothing but a black and white photograph of a baby. She lies naked on a bear skin rug, the spitting image of her mother, who was either a porpoise or a mermaid, according to family tradition. In the sky, drifting in from the distance: a giant cow's udder descends upon the city.

2

I try teaching class with a cauliflower crammed up my nostril and print all their examinations in invisible ink. But my students just yawn, and one by one float up out of their chairs towards the window. Then the foghorn blasts over the loudspeaker, and we're under the desks counting backwards on our rosaries. We know the bombers aren't *trying* to hit us. That they're just following orders from the General, who's following orders from the President, and so on up the food chain. But just the same we all feel more than a little relieved when we pick ourselves up and flash our irradiated teeth. Afterwards, my students hold hands and sing protest songs, and I know it's pointless to continue. Instead, I send everyone home with a raspberry pinned to their chest, so they at least have something to nibble on while watching the sunset through x-ray goggles.

3

It's her day off from the Sideshow, and the fat lady lies down for a nap. She dreams of lunch, and of dinner after that, the following morning's breakfast, flapjacks stacked to the ceiling, the bathtub overflowing with scrambled eggs . . . She is awakened by the clown warbling love ballads. One of his floppy shoes is caught in a beartrap; he belches a bubble with his heart inside. It beats in Morse code: Be Mine, Be Mine . . . The fat lady huffs out of bed and slams shut the window, but catches her beard over the sill. The clown is encouraged, begins to climb. He is the Prince in *Rapunzel*, ascending a tower of sausage links to his bacon-greased beloved . . . even as the tower tips, the fat lady plummets . . . the clown still climbing . . . up through clouds, past radio satellites—and here he pauses to juggle the moon and the sun—up even onto St. Peter, who's just now turning the key in the gates to Paradise.

4

Becalmed at sea. Twin chimpanzees take turns knotting pink bows in one another's back hair. Below deck the captain vomits into a pill cup. The first mate shanks golf balls from the crow's nest. The frame pans back: a fat man playing with a toy ship in the bathtub. The tub is filled with vomit; the fat man flounces his arms and vomit splashes up onto the floor forming small islands on the tile. A nude couple lying out under a polka-dot umbrella waves from one of the islands. One of the chimps waves back; the other works to hoist the sails in the hot breeze now rising as the ship lifts towards the fat man's mouth.

5

In the bakery, a girl stuffs herself with raspberry tarts. The baker tosses back his head, lifts the back of his hand to his brow. It's a bit like something out of a Greek play; and when the girl's mother pinches her thigh and takes a bite out of her ankle... If only the girl had been more attentive of her figure, or her mother more attentive to the girl—who's still a little doughy in the bosom, her mother quips. So the baker slides her back into the oven until she rises a firm, flaky crust. But the baker has neglected to lower his hand from his forehead, and the hand just sticks there, flexing, independent of the arm. Is he making a pass at her? Meanwhile, the oven's now a gigantic snowshoe tramping toward the Arctic.

6

For the past three nights a bear has knocked on my door asking to use the bathroom. "Occupied," I shout through the mail slot, "Out of order." I wonder if it's the same bear every night, or if it's a group of bears conspiring to play a little prank. Or maybe it's one of the three bears. Goldilocks not sitting quite right in Papa bear's belly, and he's not about to just squat down right there in a bush like some animal. Though now I think I remember in the end Goldilocks gets away. Slipping out Baby bear's bedroom window into the forest edging on darkness, all alone and scared out of her wits, if only for a tepid bowl of porridge and a bed that's not-quite-right . . . And here I am in my own not-quite-right bed when the knocking comes again. Tonight, my curiosity gets the best of me. "Come in, come in," I say, and in she strolls, her dress torn, platinum tresses tussled, followed by the rest of the Bear family. Why Baby Bear's cuter than a teddy in his blue overalls, and Mama wears an apron with a picture of a hen brooding on a stack of pancakes. Papa hops from foot to foot, doing a little pee-pee dance. "Down the hall to the left," I say, and I know I'm going to regret this . . . "But what the hell, why not stay the night."

7

I pull up to the diner just in time to catch a parrot holding the door for another parrot. There's a pair of deep-sea divers at the counter sipping steaming cups of coffee through their iron visors, and I'd be lying if I don't say I'm having reservations. But breakfast's a-calling and scrambled eggs and flapjacks are spilling off the gridle all over the floor. I grab a hashbrown and drift across the diner, when a gum-twirling waitress sidles up and stuffs my face with an enormous sausage link. But was one of the parrots wearing an eyepatch, or was that just a pirate with a parrot on his shoulder? No sooner do I think than my thumbs are tied to my big toes and I'm tossed overboard, and wouldn't you know I could now well believe the sun rose for a second time that morning.

8

We had to get the electric blanket to the mayor. It was the last one left in the entire country, but it was a good ten miles by carriage, through thick forest, to the capital, and the snow was really coming down. The carriage rocked and shook, and me and the driver switched places. It was nothing like you think, it was like passing through a bubble, then the bubble pops. One moment I was in the carriage, then the big black horses were straining under my hands. I was shivering, and all I kept thinking was somewhere in the capital the mayor was freezing, dying of cold, but with all this snow surely there would be no power, the electric blanket would be useless. Just an ordinary blanket. You toss it over your shoulders, then the whole dark world falls down on you.

9

I always suspected there was something odd about the neighbors, Steve and Marleen, and this morning my suspicions were confirmed, when leaving for work, I caught them wrestling on the front lawn. Marleen had Steve in a scissor lock around the waist, and Steve, squirming out of her grip, was attempting to gouge her eyes. I didn't know whether to call the police, or stay and watch, figured what the hell, and dropped an elbow on Steve's head. Who knows how far things would have gone—but around eight-thirty the sprinklers popped up, and then the school bus came rolling by to collect the chattering children that had gathered to watch. There the three of us stood, nursing black eyes and bruised ribs, watching the droplets splattering on the sidewalk and coalescing in cool little pools into which we could slither off our clothes and swim away this life.

10

The dentist probes my mouth with an octopus tentacle; his eyes are wound silk. From the cavity in my left molar he pulls: maracas, a warm bottle of milk, a chandelier and matching candelabras, a brown-bagged egg-salad sandwich I'd forgotten about since middle-school. Then there's the recipe for my grandmother's angelic angel's food cake inscribed on the underside of my tongue. This he copies down and hands to his assistant, who rolls up the paper and slides it into an alabaster jar. It's only when they walk out of the examination room arm-in-arm that I notice her jackal's head. Now, I only brush my teeth with a celery stalk, and my feet are wet leaves.

11

There comes the first real break in the heat, and all across the city they're wagging their toes out apartment windows. The firemen climb the long ladders leaned up against the sides of the buildings and count: one little piggy, two little piggy . . . All at once they sneeze, and the fairytale princess hiding out in the penthouse wakes up, complaining of a toothache. Meanwhile, a man goes from door to door begging a cup of baloney, a pinch of wolfsbane. It's not that I'm callous to the needs of others, but you can never be too cautious these days, so I tiptoe over to the door, securing the triple-chain-locks, and the deadbolt. Then I'm back out on the fire escape, watching through binoculars—the princess is up on the roof, tempting the ledge. The firemen surround the building, twirl their mustaches around their faces like clock hands. "Jump," they shout, knowing she won't. But as public servants, they strive to keep up appearances, and call in the trampoline brigade . . . For the paparazzi, of course, bouncing higher and higher above the street, camera shutters clicking, hoping to catch a shot for the rag columns.

12

He selects a stale baguette from the bakery cart and steps into the batter's box. The nose-picking gorilla on the mound winds-up windmill-style, lobs a wailing infant right over the sweet-spot of the plate. It's a high blooper into deep left, easily caught. But children can be so fussy, and the left fielder rocks the child in his arms and hums the National Anthem, the only lullaby he can think of. Then he crinkles his nose: the child has shit its diaper; and, as if in symbiosis, he too shits his pants, a brown runnel trickling down his pants leg and onto the astroturf. The players on field, the fans in the bleachers, pinch their noses, discreetly shuffle towards the first base line; and the stadium lilts, like a ship rocked by waves . . . We are adrift, says the umpire, and taking hold of the captain's wheel behind home plate, steers east, where the dark clouds lift away: then cries, "Batter-up." But now the coaches and players in the dugouts of both teams are curled up on the benches with their knees tucked to their chests, each with a peanut in his mouth which he sucks on like a pacifier.

13

The frogs fall so thick we shovel them off the driveway with giant spatulas. By noon, the plows will come careening down the street; and like always, we'll be waiting next to the mailbox to greet them, waving, smiling green smiles. The drivers can be so inconsiderate, they'll bury you up to the crown of the head, leaving you to tunnel blindly back inside though the nearest open window, flopping exhausted into bed. The blunder will only be recognized when you wake up hours later, next to the neighbor's wife; but by then the sun will be nodding off behind the mountains, and well, since you're already here, might as well stay for dinner. As always, the kitchen will be decorated like a French restaurant, and as always, you'll be naked save for a napkin knotted around your sex. Grandma and grandpa, aunts, uncles, cousins five-times removed, will be lined up to kiss you on both cheeks—but when the thin-mustached waiter sets the platter on the table and lifts the lid . . . But by now you'll have already guessed, frog's legs.

14

I stick carrots in my ears, a cucumber in each nostril. I stroke my beard and watch the sparks fly up the chimney. My brain says hungry, my stomach, read to me, and the girl in the too-short skirt and bare-it-all blouse won't have anything to do with me. I come upon a gorilla flying a kite in the rain. I unzip the zipper running down its back and out steps the same gorilla aiming a gun to its head. I try the zipper again and now the gorilla is holding a fishing pole with a banana on the line. I unzip the gorilla for a third time and we are back to the gorilla with the kite. The zipper gleams in my eye. As I reach for it I know I will be trapped in this cycle for the rest of my life.

15

The mayor's mustache slips from his upper lip and into bed with his mistress. The mistress, mistaking it for a mouse, stomps it to death under a high heel. His wife interrogates him about the missing mustache, to which the mayor mumbles something about a fire and how he saved some two dozen orphans and a couple of cats, though he was too modest to keep an exact count. The press runs with the story: Hero Mayor Saves Orphan Cats from House Fire—guaranteeing him a landslide into a second term. Meanwhile, the mistress, now recognizing what she though was a mouse for a mustache playing dirty, bends it over her knee and spanks the truth right out of it.

16

My mustache migrates south for the winter, settling just above my navel; my beard hangs down between my legs. It's a cold, clear night, and I'm out strolling in the garden admiring the Queen's dainties draped across the hedges, when a used car salesman waddles up and tries to sell me a horse. She rides just like a dream, he whispers in my ear, patting the horse on the rump. Just like a dream. But the horse is clearly on its last leg, and I tell it as much, but just as I go to tear the hangman's black hood off the salesman the horse bats its long eyelashes as if to say, "I'm sorry. Please love me".

17

In the barn the farmer uses chopsticks to pluck the eggs from beneath the hens. The surgeon, in fishnets and garter belt, operates on the roof. He slices away the gangrenous shingles and peers into the loft, catching a glimpse of the farmer's only daughter, industrious caterpillar, spinning a dress out of hay. She is beautiful, in that unpolished, forlorn way only only daughters are in fairytales . . . except for the long crone's nose hanging below her chin and tapering into a black wart. If one of the eggs should slip from the chopsticks the entire scene would be awash in yolk. So that, to see the story through to the end, you'd have to sop up this page with a giant piece of toast.

18

Moondrunk in the bath. All my toy ships have sunk. The bear on the toilet folds torn sheets of newspaper into airplanes that it flies around the bathroom. The sharp nose of one of the planes hits me in the eye. It's a fatal blow, and I sink below the water, prepared to join my armada. The bear flushes twice and exits balanced on a striped ball.

19

When a rhinoceros buries its head in the sand it shuts out the world to its ugliness. Then you can sneak up behind it with a stick, poke its rump without fear, for at most you'll be met with a half-hearted fart. Only if you snake a stethoscope backwards down into the sand and position it next to its ears, coaxing it with speeches of managerial inspiration, will its head by chance resurface. But by then it will have lost the will to charge.

20

Tonight the toads line the lake's shore like tin soldiers, and the mandolins with their upraised eyebrows, which the toads pluck with their elastic tongues whenever the moon peeks from behind the clouds. You feel a tug and the rod bends in your hand, but when you reel up the line all you've caught is your own shadow. You've hooked it right under the lip and where the dangling feet touch the water an algae blooms. And look, now the toads are wearing tuxedoes! Tell the band to strike up a waltz, then stick a pin in their breasts that puff out as they dance. They'll take off like plastic bags blown across a supermarket parking lot, just like those you remember from childhood mistaking for ghosts.

21

The doctor wedges a tongue depressor under the nail of each of my toes and fingers. Then once, twice, thrice, the mallet recoils off my head. For each lump that rises he writes another prescription. Take two of the blue pills before bed . . . But by now I'm already quite delirious. I could swear the receptionist asks for my autograph on the way out, but I'm far too humble for any pretense of celebrity. Instead, I slip her a framed 8x10, then I'm crawling across the waiting room on my belly as she calls the next patient, who politely curtsies before bringing her high heel down on my neck.

22

When I die I come back as a ghost of myself at eight years old. It is the 1980's and I haunt my eight-year-old self. If this creates a paradox, no one notices. My eight-year-old self looks at me as if I were an exotic fish in a dentist's office aquarium. He comes up to the tank and taps on the glass. The imagination goes to work. He draws a picture of me in a sombrero. I draw a picture of him in a sombrero. In his picture I have no feet. At recess we feed the seagulls the crust of his jelly sandwich. The teacher catches him talking to me and calls our mom. She picks us up early, then takes us on her knee and says, "How nice, an imaginary friend." We write a story about the other houses on the block, which are all haunted by the ghosts of other eight-year-olds. They ask if we can come out to play, and we do. We run through the backyards, through the rose hedges separating the houses. We rub our cuts together, a pact of brotherhood. But ghosts do not bleed, and I wonder how even dead I betray myself.

23

The ditches on either side of the road are filling up with dead animals. I recognize lions, foxes, bears, gorillas, and other exotic species I cannot name. They are spilling out of the ditches, onto the road. It is becoming difficult to steer around them. Sirens blare in my rearview, but there is no place to pull over. I finally stop right there in the middle of the road. "License and registration," the officer demands. "But the animals," I stammer. He just stares straight down at me like I'm some lunatic. Though I offer no resistance, he pulls me roughly from the car and tosses me in the back of his cruiser. The wall of animals is rising all around us; I can no longer see the sky through the bars on the window. Again I scream I have done nothing wrong, but the bodies of the animals are pressing against the cruiser, I can see my face reflected in the many eyes. "Drive," I shout up to the officer, "drive", but the officer tilts back his head and howls, then leans down on the accelerator, without shifting the cruiser out of park. The engine heat and the smell of the animals seeps into the cabin. The cage grows smaller, the staring eyes of the animals . . .

24

An island of old men floats across the lake. I hop from head to head, using them like stepping stones, to cross to the opposite shore. Their beards are lilypads; whenever one of the old men opens his mouth a toad crawls out onto his lilypad beard. If you look closely into their eyes you will see the tadpoles racing around the lazy pupils. The island is one old man and all of the old men – all old men. The shrunken grandfather asleep in the bed he will die in every child at one time or another faintly recalls kissing lightly on his nose then hooking a pinky finger all the way up the nostril and yanking out the shriveled soul dressed in inside-out pajamas.

25

Out the kitchen window, beyond even the frontier of the swimming pool: the Jolly Rodger flies. The patch-eyed pirate, astride a giant walrus, raises, then lowers his saber—a volley of crows erases the sky. The dish you are washing slips from your hands . . . You wait for the crash . . . An hour later you are waiting still. The maid sweeps the floor and up the wall; she continues across the ceiling— and now the descending dust bunnies have made a warren of your hair. Behind you, posed sage-like on the edge of the countertop: a grocer weighs a cauliflower on the tip of his tongue.

26

It is quiet in the confessional, so the priest composes his memoirs. He gives puppet shows at nine and six. The wise men are old socks decorated with rusted bottlecaps; the Moses marionet has a cotton ball beard. On the other side of the screen his guardian angel sips hemlock from a silver flask. Critiques his manuscript. "I walked across all of San Francisco with the Baptist's gangrenous big toe in a shoebox." The stained-glass saints are dressed as 1930's gangsters; they step out of the tableaus firing their tommy guns into the ceiling. Mary, breasts bared, bangs her head against the altar. The only light comes from the moon climbing out of her mouth.

27

An old woman mounts the seesaw and shouts, *giddyup*! She gallops around the playground where an old man scoops handfuls of sand into a red pail. Something about the motion of the seesaw makes him curious, and grabbing his ankles, he lifts his feet above his head and rocks back and forth on his bottom, tipping into the hole in the sand. The seesaw bucks the old woman who lands on top of the old man, housedress flipping up over her head. "Why Norman, I never knew you cared . . ." And now another old man, for modesty's sake, shuffles over in an open bathrobe and fills in the hole. Two widowers whirling on the merry-go-round shed layers of clothes like temperamental toddlers, fly up conjoined like mating dragonflies spinning splattering on the windshields of speeding cars, startling the nonagenarian grunting out chin-ups on the monkey bars. After years of climbing, I have finally reached the summit of the slide, and look out, smiling, a sagging heaviness spreading in my diaper, just happy to be alive.

28

I sat at the back of the bus next to a severed thumb. Everyone was complementing the thumb on its remarkable hairdo. I had to agree, it was a remarkable hairdo; in fact, we all had remarkable hairdos. We decided to play a game: at every stop we would exchange hairdos. I ended up with a 50's flattop, and the thumb, an old woman's blue beehive. The old woman had a slicked back ponytail, slightly thinning on top. When I got off, I headed to the post office to mail a letter. The post office had just unveiled a new series of stamps dedicated to people with remarkable hairdos. There was Jennifer Aniston, Elvis, Trump . . . I looked down at the letter, it was addressed to the old woman. I opened it and read: "Dear Snowflake, Many a-night have I lay awake dreaming of you at the beauty parlor, in curlers under the hot drier, flipping through yellowed issues of *People* . . ." It was signed with a thumb print over which some of the ink had smudged into what looked like an afro.

29

When the first slant of dawn ekes through the blinds the shadow awakens, unfurls from underneath its sleeper down the bed across the carpet up the wall. Outside, the trees are full of women's white gloves. A little girl stands on the corner cradling the head of a doll. Meanwhile, the shadow slips under the door, no longer defined by the contours of the body. There's a hearse parked on the front lawn. The shadow slithers into the passenger's seat. The driver is the little girl, who now has the head of the doll. Her real head sits on the console between them; instead of eyes, bronze doorknobs.

30

An apron run amok. Playing Tarzan from the ceiling fan. Its housewife straddling the toaster. Naked save for a pair of ovenmitts, cinnamon bun areoles and spatula crotch. The milkman spying through the window knows only so much as he lets on. The dead borrow under the azalea garden, their teeth of stained playing cards. Canoes paddle across the night, ferrying the stars.

31

There's a miniature sabretooth tiger thawing from an ice cube on the counter and a wheelchair with a warm drink. There's a rat gnawing at the wheelchair tire, its air-bloat belly. Inside the ice the tiger flexes a muscle; the rat floats up towards the ceiling. There's something pre-historic about the apartment, the guests swaggering simian-like, swigging their beer bottles then swinging them like caveman clubs at the rat's primeval piñata: and there's a woman outside the window looking in, thinking just this. Though this could just be the woman, who wasn't invited to the party in the first place, sulking in her bitterness. Because, honestly, aren't you too even a little curious? The drink left on the wheelchair, now on the verge of tipping. The sabretooth tiger, its story . . .

32

Hands crossed over her chest, an old woman lies half-buried in a sandbox. Between her legs, a mousetrap; safety pins through the nipples of her deflated breasts. The fat spiders that live in her armpits work to unweave their webs: corpses of houseflies, rats' skeletons, the broken tiles of mosaics that were once the pupils in the eyes of saints. An old man has lost so much of his mind his hat falls completely over his head. His sex a stalk of broccoli, the sprouts grafted to the grey pubic hairs. Once, on a wartime winter's day, the two had met. Hand in hand, they had gone for a walk in the forest, their footfalls in the fresh snow the blasts of trumpets.

33

Somewhere in the city an ear canal ruptures, wax everywhere, covering the cars, the buildings, thigh-high in the streets, toddlers with toy shovels and bright orange pails building castles in the mess. A clown trips on stage, off go his floppy shoes. But where are his feet? His big red nose rolls to the edge of the stage—his body deflates as if someone had pulled the plug of an innertube. Eight spider's legs grow out of his wig, which scuttles about like a wind-hassled flame. Everyone in the audience is wearing their pajamas, except me—dressed all in black, I rappel down from the ceiling and retrieve the clown's white cotton gloves. Later, back at home, I display then in a silver cage above a plaque labeled: MATING DOVES.

34

There's a clown in every class. In our case, he teaches it. Yesterday, we learned to ride a unicycle while juggling bowling balls; today, the joy buzzer gag. Later: balloon animals. "Will this be on the final," asks braces in the front row, pulling the whoopee cushion from her seat, and is belted with a cream pie. Mother asks, "How was school today," and I pull a bouquet of plastic flowers from my sleeve: she tacks them up on the refrigerator next to my A+ history report on P.T. Barnum. On the day before summer break, he swings in through the window on a rope of knotted handkerchiefs, slipping on a banana peel. Then he takes the eraser from the blackboard and whooshes himself away.

35

Inside the monster I found a machine that made other monsters. It looked like a cow's udder in comic nose and glasses like the bumbling lead in a Vaudeville act would wear. The udder churned and the nose sneezed and a smaller monster shot out one of the nostrils. This morning, I show you the tiny monster splayed out on the couch where it had landed in the night. But even then you refuse to believe me, as if for the world you'd forgotten all about monsters.

36

Waiting at the bus stop: a cow in a butcher's smock. It stands on its hind-legs. On the smock there is a silhouette of another cow diagramed into its edible parts. Every time the cow lows, the doily around its neck gathers another fringe; a spark fires in the fuse screwed into its head. Whenever the milkman, on his back under the cow, tugs one of the udders, the cow rises a little higher off the sidewalk. Indeed: it's well on its way to the next stage of transcendence—a scrap of flotsam tailing the clouds; a leather satchel for angels; a zeppelin kept afloat by four bloated stomachs . . .

37

One of the apes digs the graves, the other lays down inside with its long arms crossed over its chest. Then they switch. There's another ape who inscribes the names on the tombstones, has a toothache, can't see so well out of its left eye. It is what is, it's a living. Beats the zoo, the circus. The trouble is so few people die anymore. All you have to do is pop a pill and you go on living. The graveyard manager stops paying the apes, they're starving, they argue when one of the apes sneaks off behind the mausoleum and smokes the last cigarette. The ape with the bad eye spanks the other two over the head with the shovel and buries them in one of the graves. Then gets lonely, overcome with guilt, steals the revolver from the bottom draw of the graveyard manger's desk and blows its brains out. The trouble is so few people die anymore. Only apes . . . and there goes the last of them.

38

The boys are taught to play fight with real knives. Father rides a unicycle around the backyard while juggling cucumbers. Mother holds an umbrella over her head waiting for the rain to come, which it does, but only under the umbrella. One of the boys slips up and draws blood, and a black tongue of lightening licks down, firing the filaments of her hair. So that, for an instant, you can see the eyes on the cucumbers.

39

My dead grandfather is flying a kite over a field. He is moving farther and farther into the distance, towards the horizon and the beautiful blue hills that lay like the knees of a crouching giant. The kite rises, but so does the giant, a lumbering creature out of myth, tearing away a whole patch of the sky. But my grandfather is still running across the field with the limp string in his hand. Though he is far away I can see his face, it is not the face of the grandfather I knew but the one I had seen only in pictures from his army days, before he met my grandmother. He looks so happy, I have never seen him so happy, disappearing into a black hole through which I could die once and never again.

40

Right on time the delivery boy slips the monkey through the mail slot. But when I go to retrieve the tire pump, to reinflate the monkey, there's Grandma curled up in the trunk. She's sleeping so soundly, I really shouldn't wake her, but I've got important business with that monkey, so out the old witch goes . . . down the hill and through the doors of the old church. The monkey is at the lectern, thumping the Good News in one paw, in the other, the tire pump . . . Then all of the sudden we're wrestling on the altar, and out of nowhere Grandma comes up from behind and gets me in a scissor lock. For 93 she has the stamina of a tiger. Could it be the brown pills she takes for her arthritis? The congregation in the pews roars, and when they go for the double team, I know I'm done for. And I think, isn't this just like one of those times when mother would snatch away the remote and say, alright, that's enough, time for bed.

41

I catch the dog trying on one pair of underwear over another. Grey briefs, frilly panties, polka-dotted granny bloomers, they're all bunched up about Ollie's mid-section and he's walking on his hind-legs around the bedroom as if to show off his new trick. But that isn't my underwear, which is neatly folded in my top dresser draw. Is he stealing from the neighbors when I let him out at night to shit? I think, when the dog—a big ol' Great Dane who comes up to my waist on all fours—places a huge paw on either shoulder and slobbers all over my face. Ok, boy, but you need to give those back right now. But now the underwear has vanished . . . and where's his tail? I feel a breeze stirring up behind me and I almost know when I reach back to confirm . . . Though that still doesn't answer the question of where all that underwear could have gone.

42

In the pet shop window, I see a gerbil wearing tiny frilly underpants, a dog in rimless glasses, a parakeet with a mohawk. My landlord doesn't allow pets, but I feel I'm meant to choose one . . . But now I'm in the window too, my hands pressed against the glass, naked save for an "Adopt Me" sign over my understandably shriveled penis. There's a little girl in front of the shop tugging at her father's jacket, she's crying and pointing at me . . . I don't fit into the carry-along, so they drag me through the streets on a leash. It's cold, and I'm miserably embarrassed, but I have hope that where I'm headed is nicer than my cramped one-room flat. An old granny hobbles past on a cane. She doubles behind and spanks my naked ass. "Nice buns, hot stuff!", and now I'm being dragged in the opposite direction. The little girl comes up and kicks her in the shin. Granny crumbles, then pops up and socks her in the nose. I think this is my chance and make a break for it. But I'm back in the pet shop window between the gerbil and the dog. There's a little girl out front, she's crying and pointing at me . . .

43

I lie back in the dentist's chair. "I want the canines done in silver," I mumble through a mouth stuffed with cotton balls, but the dentist fills the cavity in my left molar with what tastes like grape marmalade. When I protest, his inflatable assistant presses the gas mask down over my face. I dream of my childhood living room, the hump-backed television is filling with snow, snow is spilling off the screen, I'm buried up to neck in it. I spit my teeth out one by one, they lie on the snow like rodent-sized grave markers. There's a fruit bowl filled with halved clams, a chemist's phial of red ants on an instrument tray. The dentist sits cross-legged on the snowed-over mound of the couch, kissing my mother's goosepimpled neck. He sees that I see and reaches towards me, pinching my nose in the claw of his middle and index fingers, like a jesting uncle. "This won't hurt a bit, sport," he says, lifting it off my face.

44

Nights I wear a white sheet with holes cut out for eyes and haunt the moon. One time, I woke up in the pants pocket of a giant; another, a tiny meteor left a fist-shaped crater in my chest. The moon men have twenty-seven toes, three on each of their nine tentacles, and are extremely ticklish when afraid. The best ideas are almost always tri-angular in shape, or sometimes three-dimensional cubes, and are most often found under broken flowerpots, baited in mousetraps you'd set years earlier then completely forgot about until they snap at you.

45

Bride and groom trapeze artists swing from opposite ends of the cathedral, meeting over the altar in a kiss. "I now pronounce you . . ." stammers the priest, cracking the ring master's whip. A trampoline, followed by twin coffins, is wheeled down the center aisle. They bounce off the former, summersaulting into the latter, living out their whole lives in the span. "How time flies," weep the clowns in black mourning skirts, smearing their bright makeup, and pile in on top. The strong man, a coffin heft on either shoulder, marches off to the grave-yard. ". . . and dust to dust," stumbles the priest, who's also a doctor, delivering the fat lady's even fatter baby right there on the altar, then spanking its bright bottom.

46

I hadn't seen my auntie in years, so when she suddenly invited me to dinner I didn't know what to expect. What I *didn't* expect was that she'd become a horse. I don't mean to imply that she was fat. Though she had always been a bit on the tubby side. But, aside from the floral housedress and wide-rimmed glasses, she was distinctly equine. "So auntie, how's Uncle Ernie?" She bucked, upending the bowl of gold-foil wrapped caramels. I'd forgotten Uncle Ernie had made a fortune in made-to-order prosthetics then blew it all on a waitress he'd met on a sales trip to Des Moines. "Mother sends her regards," I lied. The two hadn't spoken since the "incident" at grandmother's funeral. She pawed at the carpet, then back-kicked her hooves through the glass front plate of the antique clock. This was going nowhere. I needed a new approach. Then I saw the saddle hung next to the door. . .

All night we rode, to a tune of boastful braying. All night we rode, inside a teacup murdering the sun.

47

I leave the bath running and check the soup reheating on the stove. When I get back to the bathroom, the door is locked and water is running out underneath into the hall. I go back to the kitchen, to get a knife to jimmy the lock, and there's a bird perched on the handle of the soup pot. It's the same bird I shooed off the mailbox this morning. The same bird that has come to shit there every day this week. I wade back to the living room, through water up to my knees, and on the old Tiffany lamp in the corner is that same bird. I go back to the kitchen. The bird is still on the pot handle. But now there's another of the same bird on the sink faucet. I head back to the living room. The water is up to my armpits, so I don't so much walk as propel myself along with an astronaut's slow zero-g strides. There on the TV, the curtain rods, in the floral design of the wallpaper. It's the same bird! The same bird! The world is over and over becoming the same bird and the water is rising in the flood that will start everything all over again.

48

In her final days, Grandma swept the floors in her wedding gown. Under the veil: a birdhouse or sometimes a clock. Grandpa, ten years dead, lay pantsless on the couch. When the clock struck noon he sat bolt upright and demanded, "What's for lunch?" Then a fat rat would whistle out of the birdhouse dressed as the pizza delivery boy. Grandma would set a hot slice on Grandpa's lap, at which he would fart a cloud of dust and crumble back down. Outside, a storm had just past and the children were rolling around in the mudholes costumed as merry little hogs.

49

The line to ride the electric chair spilled out of the prison and into the courtyard. The judge handed out sentences from behind an ironing board. Mother served snacks on the roof so we could watch the rolling blackouts. That winter the town had filled in the public pool with plans to build a new Mega Church. But nothing ever came of it. Still, on those eternal summer afternoons, you could sometimes hear the immortal cry of "Canon ball."

50

Once I was a circus acrobat. I swung stillborn from my mother's womb by the umbilical cord wrapped around my neck. My hands were flashlights. I waved my flashlight hands over the astonished faces of the crowd as I circum-ambulated the Big Top tent. Then one day the strongman standing on the shoulders of another strongman standing on the back of an elephant grabbed me by the ankles as the tightrope walker cut the umbilical cord with garden sheers. My face turned from blue, to red, to pink. Later on, I hitched a ride in the back of the clown car on my way to wherever it is the unexpected go when they're unexpected.

51

A pile of feathers unhatching into egg. Toothpicks of carved baby bones displayed in a smoke shop window. I ladle the contents of my head into the bowl set before me and leave it on the table to cool. Later in the night I come downstairs and begin to spell, a wizard conjuring his cruel curses into a lighted window. The next morning, I call in sick to work. But I am talking into a pinecone.

52

The zoo has adopted a new kangaroo. I press through the crowd to get right up close to the cage. The kangaroo is crouched near the back corner, half concealed in shadow. It looks sick and holds out a tin alms cup. I guess in these dark times everyone's feeling the crunch, I think, and search my pocket for something to contribute. But all I find is this spare bellybutton, slightly larger than a dime. I pass my thumb over the bellybutton, wiping away a dusting of blueish lint, mesmerized in its whorls; when I notice something moving in the kangaroo's pouch. It's a baby, diapered in a pauper's grimy rags; it crawls out of the pouch, across the floor of the cage, pressing its face to the bars. I look from the baby to the bellybutton to the baby. The baby has a bellybutton on the center of its forehead, between its eyebrows . . . That's when the zookeeper grabs me by the arm and escorts me to the exit. "You can't provoke the animals," he reprimands. "I was only trying to help," I say.

53

Somewhere between the moon and heaven: a man bites into the flank of a cow. Just like that, everything changes. The butcher weeps at his own superfluousness, cuts another slice of flesh from his arm. Housewives line up into the street to fill their purses with the wax-paper-wrapped parcels. Lovers picnicking in a monastery pull from their basket: an alchemist's phial of bee stings, the sea breaking in a glass globe. When they finish, they roll up the leftovers in a blanket of mishmashed constellations; then think to stay a while longer and enjoy each other. "Blasphemy," cries the Abbot, swinging a flyswatter. They jump out the only window looking towards the light, falling for what seems like hours. Land on an island rising in a bowl of soup, decide here someday their children's children will grow old.

54

We carried out all we could from under the skirts of the old women, then headed south. But either someone had pinched together the floor and the ceiling, or else the windows had been installed inside-out, so we had to walk on our elbows the rest of the way. I weep even now at all the soft-boiled eggs we left behind, and the story was so commonplace we had to invent certain facts just to prove the lie. Which is fine, if you get your kicks stealing the padded seats off unicycles from under clowns with hemorrhoids. But since then I've reformed, only practice acupuncture to straighten the spines of dictionaries, and even carry an hourglass in my pocket on the end of a thin gold chain.

55

The constellation of the farmer milks the swollen udder bag of the moon: thus moonbeams and angels and the soft blue glow of lakes. An ape uses an old man's suspenders to hold up its rain boots; the old man, in turn, pays the ape a peanut to turn cartwheels in the mud. A mouse crawls into your ear as you sleep, navigating the synaptic maze of your brain: that night you dream only of platers of exotic cheeses. Just as a man is sitting down to supper his tongue falls onto the dinner plate. He jabs it with his fork and the tongue wriggles and squirms. And the farmer milks the udder bag of the moon and in the cool pale glow the cows low on into morning.

56

Thumbs in navels, the children float around the pool on their backs. "Your daiquiri, sir," says one of the parents, "and a Pina colada for you, madam," tipping the straw to her bubble-gum smacked lips. You might stub your toe on a diamond ring lost in the grass, and think: someone loves me. And it might well be true. But there's a porpoise in the water, and it surfaces under one of the children, and then another. Their bathing suits bloat with bubbles, and they rise, hovering in the middle-air, pudgy little parade balloons. But what goes up, must come down, and it's getting on towards supper, then bedtime. Drawing the feathered shafts from the quivers, the parents lock them in their sights.

57

Maybe it was the atmosphere, or maybe we were all a bit giddy, but every fifteen seconds or so someone would stab me in the thigh with a hatpin and hand me a drink. But then, why were these razor blades scotch taped to my nipples? And who was it suggested we kill ourselves, anyway? Luckily, we spent all our bullets polishing our eyebrows before noticing none of the waiters had feet. Though it *might* have been the atmosphere, because suddenly we were floating up over our bodies and bumping up against the ceiling. It all has something to do with oxygen leaving the brain, and from where I stood I looked a shade green. Or maybe we *had* killed ourselves, for all our fine conversation, and we were just living out the afterlife of some brat's pet goldfish . . . When, just like that, someone clicks off the TV.

58

Under a rock a monk fondles his prayer-beads. He's afraid of the sunlight through which I ride a camel down the narrow streets of Istanbul, a shoe dangling from my left ear. With each step we rise further into the sky: from here I can see the Butcher's stall: the Butcher's blood-bright belly is shaking with laughter. And all the children running around as if without a care: don't they know people are sleeping in the apartments upstairs. But wait, those aren't children at all, but old men who've forgotten how to lace up their beards.

59

She bends the boy over her knee and spanks him once, then again. The boy hiccups: a tire iron, a box kite, a diamond ring inside a soap bubble. The bubble pops, and now the boy is on one knee, fitting the ring to her finger. The other children giggle, singing "Johnny loves teacher, Johnny loves teacher," and line up with their permission slips—travelers presenting their passports at the border to some long-desired country. But in the tiny glossy photos one child has a mustache, another's missing teeth have been colored in with a green crayon. They're obviously fakes. They'll have to be detained. Then sent to their rooms without supper.

60

A runaway car crashes through the TV set into my living room tailed by a caravan of sirens and lights that set the furniture aflame. The officers step out of their vehicles and point their guns to their heads. I look through the windshield of the car being chased and see that the driver has my face. So I slip off my shoes and quietly tiptoe upstairs into bed. The moon reaches through the window and takes what it may. I must have fallen asleep before the shooting began because the last thing I remember is being captain of a pirate ship crewed by apes. When I creep back downstairs all the policemen's eyebrows have been shaved.

61

The movie hadn't started yet so me and Janice were going at it in the back row. Suddenly, the lights dimmed, the projector rolled. It was a film of me and Janice kissing, done in arthouse black and white, like a home movie. The audience complained, several people left the theater in outrage. The raucous teenager in the row in front of ours turned around and spat, "pathetic." I had to agree, seeing it like this, it wasn't exactly flattering. And I think Janice saw it too, because she suddenly grabbed the boy around the shoulders and kissed him. Fervently. Passionately. Like she never kissed me. From afar, I saw the camera crew roll into position, the director snap "action." From afar, I am falling backwards, down a long dark aisle towards a light that is the moon crashing into my face.

62

The TV weatherman points to a picture of a cloud with two black eyes. I remove the frozen turkey from my own bruised eye, slap it on the table for Grandma to carve. "A leg for Father and another for Uncle Marvin, and breasts for you, my dear," and she leans over double so her breasts spill out of her apron onto my plate. Everyone has taken off their astronaut helmets to eat and I know I'm supposed to say something . . . when suddenly the weatherman steps right out of the screen and punches Grandma square in the jaw.

63

It is time to cut the cake, but bride and groom are nowhere to be found. The bathrooms are searched, under the tables, the DJ calls for them over the loudspeaker. But it's such a beautiful cake, the baker has truly outdone himself, so huge the life-size man and wife topper almost touches the ceiling of the reception hall. The guests work together stacking the chairs. The father of the bride, nearly trampling the maids of honor, claims the right, and balanced on the top chair he revs up the chainsaw. But now there are flies everywhere, swarming over the flower centerpieces, laying their larvae in the icing . . .

64

In my childhood bedroom my parents are diapering a giant papier-mâché squid. They are the age they were when I was just an infant, and coo softly as they work. I look around the room: those are *my* toys, *my* crib, I shout, lunging between them. But I am surprised at how warm it is, close up to the squid, which though constructed of gluey strips of newspaper squirms and struggles on the table. How its tentacles touch every part of my body at once, without shame, without suspicion it could want anything than this touching. My parents have secured the diaper flaps, and I am holding a gold safety pin long as my forearm. Then I see the squid's single enormous eye, like a runny egg in the center of its head. I look from the eye, to the ecstatic faces of my parents, to the pin's sharp point glinting . . .

65

I'm asked to check my squirt pistol at the door and even submit to the navel swab for contraband. But it's such a *small* shoe, and she's such a *large* woman, that when she disappears up to the frosted crown of her hair I forget myself and approach the stage with an outstretched hand. I'm tackled immediately, of course, by a greasy man in a sleeveless black t-shirt with the word LEFT tattooed on his right arm. Well, thank you very much, I say, but I'll see myself out, teasing at the thread of the seam running down his back. When out tumbles an ice-cream truck, the Golden Gate Bridge, and I realize after all this is just part of the demonstration, I'm riding on the back of a beautiful black horse hijacked by a burnt cup of coffee.

More and more now the day begins with a falling out of the sky into a stranger's bed. Without even thinking to pick the shingles out of your teeth you roll over and smother someone else's wife with your hot breath. But now the damn seagull nesting on your head will not stop squawking until you've knotted its wings under your chin and threatened to wear it as a bonnet. The downstairs is a ripening orchard; if you give the dull-witted grocer who's set up his stand in front of the tallest tree a good bop on the head, he'll present you with an orange big as a beach ball. But don't unpeel it just yet. It's best to wait until the gull has fallen asleep before carefully unzipping its beak and piercing the rind, sipping up the nectar as if through a funnel.

67

All the men in the photo have knotted their mustaches into bowties: the women's eyelashes are cockroach legs. The enormous fruit bowl in the background has been crudely sketched in, as if an afterthought—and this reminds you, you must vacuum out the ice box before the grocery boy arrives. But when you throw back the lid, instead of the aisle upon aisle of boxes of frozen peas, you discover a stairwell descending into the basement you never knew you had, given you live on the 15th floor of your apartment building. Each step is steeper than the one above, and when you finally arrive at the last you have to carefully lower yourself down hanging from the tips of your fingers, then drop out onto the roof, where the clouds gather thick as mousse. So you can't see the icicles forming on the tip of your nose.

68

My son is telling me about something that happened on the class trip or at the Little League game or about Tuesday's math test that he completely forgot to study for and so would I please just sign above the D before mom finds out. I'm tuned out, drowning my thoughts in a cool bowl of Frosted Flakes. Because "They're Great," says the Tiger. My psychiatrist says it's perfectly normal for a man of my age and middling social standing to indulge in occasional delusions of fancy. But my delusions take the form of a blue goldfish swimming among the soggy flakes. "And then," my son says, "right there in front of the entire class, Miss Gumble slipped . . ." I'm slipping now, deeper into the blue goldfish, happy to be a blue goldfish, happily swimming among the sparkling clusters of malted corn. Tiny islands on which one could pull up a lounge chair and bask in the gauzy blue light that lights all my best memories. Goldfish, you know, only have a memory span of about 9 seconds. So I guess I have only 8, 7, 6 . . . to explain to my son about his father, how at just around his age he learned to grow fins and breathe underwater, swim in the looming presence of a cartoon Tiger who for all I know is about to pounce off the front of the box and chase him out the kitchen, and me happy, forgetting.

69

I'm out for a walk to break in my new shoes. The shoes follow near at my heels. You have to work the leather, really soften it up, give it the chance to breath. A steady panting, coming up from behind, as I pick up the pace . . . What people don't realize is the domestic shoe is a stickler for structure. So once they're good and broken in, you need to establish a routine. Seven O'clock, right on after supper, a nice stroll around the community . . . Say hello to Bob and Randy, Martha and Bill . . . Hell, seems like the whole neighborhood's out tonight, the soft glow of the streetlights flickering on, the new moon rising over the rooftops, the shoes howling . . .

70

It is so pleasant down by the lake. Mothers come at twilight pushing strollers. "It is such a wonderful age," I say, smiling at one of the passing women. The baby pulls a revolver from its diaper. The gun is almost as big as itself, but the child aims it straight at me. "Bang, your dead, your dead." I roll to the ground in play. Or have I really been shot? Without a word, the woman wheels the stroller right over me. Now I really *am* hurt. Blood trickles down my face, it tastes sweet, like maple syrup. I can see the ducks circling in the water, bathing their feathers, exploding into bright atoms.

71

It was a sultry late summer afternoon and the ants were everywhere. I had already smooshed several, when I heard the voice. "That's a boy, son, you show 'em." Dad? But he died the year after mom passed. I felt an itching crawling up my forearm, but checked the impulse to swat at it. It was an ant, but its tiny head was my father's. The same neat mustache. That toupee. There was a group of them swarming by my feet, and I bent down to investigate. Mom, Grandpa? Aunt Esther...? "You always were a bad egg, Steward . . ." came the smoke-tinted, reproaching voice that haunted my childhood, and the ant with my aunt's face twitched its antennae in what I'm convinced was a dirty gesture. They were working together carrying the crushed ant-corpse of my Uncle Philip towards a small mound beneath the crack of the pantry door. Then I checked under my sneaker . . . I never gave much credence to the arguments for reincarnation. Though it's hard to escape the notion that you'll eventually get what's coming to you in whatever it is that comes after. I could not help musing, reaching for the can of bug spray.

72

We were square dancing under a late August moon. My high school gym teacher was calling the steps. "Promenade and do-se-do," and around we went, so that we were all just a tangle of each other's parts. I was a grown man, but I was suddenly embarrassed at being made to perform like this. My hands were sweating. Or was it her hands, or his? We were all a-tangle, as the dance quickened, coach's voicing crackling over the P.A. His angry voice. He was always angry. "Collins, you damn spaz," as the older boys pulled my jock up over my head. But if I could just free my hand from the tangle, because now I could see the stitches running over the moon's Frankenstein face. If only I could reach up and tease out one of the threads, feel the seams unravel, the moon crumble into a thousand bright little rocks that falling would all at once bring everything to a stop.

73

He turns the crank on the suitcase and watches the clothes float up and dance over the bed. Through the window cut into the bottom he can see down into the hotel boiler room, where the janitor pounds clouds into shape over a giant anvil, up to the penthouse, where the eagles lay their enormous eggs. The minibars in all the rooms are stocked with cheap schnapps, and they're free to drink, until your diaper is soaked with piss. The bellhop can smell it from the lobby, and then he's banging at the door with an outstretched palm. Instead, you tickle his head with a feather duster, then kiss him square on the mouth.

We are about to pull the plug on the ventilator when grandpa jumps up out of bed. "I've seen the Otherside, and she ain't pretty," he stammers, streaking down the hall, wrinkled ass cheeks jiggling out the open back of his gown. He bites one of the orderlies on the ankle making his escape, and the nurse is so terrified she trips backwards over his catheter tube out the window of his fifth-floor room. Luckily, she's a busty lass, rebounding off an ambulance roof with a reverberating *thunk*. But we have other problems—the funeral was prepaid! Being the youngest of the nine brothers, I slide underneath the sheets. "Oh, the extremes of frugality," and "All's well that ends well," I think. My mother has the most radiant smile as she brings the pillow down over my face . . .

75

I am exploring Mars in my childhood snowsuit. The Martians, out of the frame, plotting in their couch cushion forts, pelt me with ice cream sandwiches. My mother is in the kitchen, humming the theme to her favorite soap opera. My father walks through the door, dressed as one of the Martians. "Take me to your leader," he says, unscrewing his head. "The President's out today," I say, and unscrew mine. Then we swap. This all takes place in black and white, with subtitles in Martian. I squint to read the squiggly hieroglyphs running underneath my feet, but am I looking out through my eyes on my father's shoulders or my father's eyes on a body that is now much too small for me?

About the author

Justin Hollis has an MFA from Hofstra University and currently teaches language and literature at Palm Beach State College. His work has appeared in *Action Spectacle, Chiron Review, Cholla Needles, Corpus Callosum, Eunoia Review, GAS: Poetry, Art, and Music, Home Planet News, Main Street Rag, Querencia Press Quarterly Anthology,* and *Superpresent.*

www.ingramcontent.com/pod-product-compliance
Lightning Source LLC
Chambersburg PA
CBHW061041050726
47592CB00004B/1534